ISBN 978-1-332-53934-5
PIBN 10102730

# 1 MONTH OF FREE READING

at

## www.ForgottenBooks.com

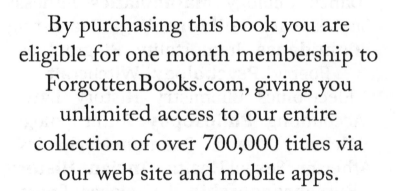

By purchasing this book you are eligible for one month membership to ForgottenBooks.com, giving you unlimited access to our entire collection of over 700,000 titles via our web site and mobile apps.

To claim your free month visit:
www.forgottenbooks.com/free102730

Fitch, J.H.

A century of

educational progress in New Brunswick

# A CENTURY

OF

# Educational Progress

IN

# New Brunswick

# 1800—1900

## J. H. FITCH

An abstract of a Dissertation presented in partial fulfilment of the requirements for the degree of Doctor of Pedagogy in the University of Toronto.

# A Century of Educational Progress in New Brunswick

## From 1800 to 1900

The history of education in New Brunswick falls conveniently into three periods. The first period, from 1800 to 1846, was a time when the schools were being established, and a system of education was developed with a minimum of administrative machinery. From 1847 to 1870 was a period of reorganization. When it came to an end, so also did the effort to support schools by voluntary assessment. The third period, from 1871 to 1900, deals with the development under the free school system.

An effort is made to show in each of the three periods the progress made in education generally, and the origin of New Brunswick's different types of schools. For the sake of continuity, each type of school is treated separately.

When New Brunswick was founded in 1784, the Royal Instructions to Governor Thomas Carleton commanded that the Province be divided into counties, and the latter into parishes. The parish was a civil unit from the first, and the name was used in the same sense as township. The Instructions also provided a plot of land in each parish for the support of the school master, and another section stated that school masters from England must be licensed by the Lord Bishop of London, and native teachers by the Governor. Before 1800 there were very few schools, and fewer good teachers. The best teachers were those sent out from England by the Society for the Propagation of the Gospel in Foreign Parts, which gave a small grant to maintain them. There were a few private schools in St. John, and an occasional one elsewhere.

**1800—1846**
**Parish Schools.** It was not until 1802 that the Legislature succeeded in passing an Act to give money from the Provincial Treasury for the support of schools. The first grant was £420 to be apportioned by the Courts of General Sessions, so that £10 would be applied to the aid of a school in each parish, "in such manner as shall best assist in maintaining such schools as may be already established, or as shall induce the establishing of other schools where they may judge the same necessary." Nothing was said about the cost of housing the school, nor about additional pay for the teacher. These expenses were met by subscription among the inhabitants. The apportioning of the Legislative grant was left to the Courts of General Sessions. One of these bodies presided over each county, and was composed of Justices of the Peace, one from each parish. The parish was the unit for administering the elementary school, and continued to be until free schools came in.

In 1816 an interesting piece of legislation permitted Parish Schools to be supported by taxation. This feature did not meet with popular approval, and no schools were thus supported. In 1818 the provision was repealed. Another section of the Act of 1816, which authorized the Courts of General Sessions to appoint two School Trustees for each parish, was continued.

The number of Parish School Trustees was increased to three in 1833, and they were made regular parish officers. The duties of the Trustees were becoming more strenuous. They were required to divide the parishes into school districts, and to inspect the schools. The Trustees made out a certificate showing the number of schools kept in each parish, the number of scholars, their sex and ages, and the amount subscribed by the inhabitants. The Trustees sent their certificates to the Courts of General Sessions, which in turn made a compilation of these reports for the Lieutenant Governor.

The teachers were required to furnish the Clerks of the Peace with an account of the number of male and female scholars, with names and ages. They did this every six months,

2

the usual length of time for a teacher to remain in one school. Half the teacher's salary was derived from the Legislative grant of £10 for six months, which was paid if the inhabitants had subscribed an equal amount. This obligation the inhabitants usually discharged by furnishing the teacher with board and lodging, a pernicious practice called "boarding around."

New arrangements for Parish Schools were made in 1837. A Board of Education was appointed for each county. The Boards consisted of three persons chosen by the Governor in Council. Instead of having control of the schools in a county, as might have been expected, these Boards were created solely for the purpose of examining candidates for teacher's license. They did not issue the licenses, but merely reported upon the suitability of the candidates to the Lieutenant Governor, who issued them. The licenses were valid in the county for which they were issued.

No further changes were made in the arrangements for Parish Schools during the period under review.

**Madras Schools.** The Society for the Propagation of the Gospel in Foreign Parts had introduced the National System into New Brunswick as early as 1786. In places where a large number of pupils could be assembled, the monitorial arrangement was admirably suited to the needs of a people who could not afford to pay much for their schools. In 1820 the Madras Board was incorporated in New Brunswick, and given an annual grant of £500 from the Provincial Treasury. The schools operated by the Board taught elementary subjects and the Catechism and other religious doctrines of the Church of England, so that the Board attracted the gifts of wealthy people who saw in it an agency, not only for the education of the young along the usual lines, but in religion as well. Being well endowed, the Madras Board was able to make fairly large grants to its schools, as is shown by the following extract from the Report of the Madras Schools in 1820.

3

Grant to the Madras School at Fredericton ............. .. £100

" " .. " Kingston ....... .........£ 60

" " " Gagetown ................£ 40

" " Sussex Vale .. .. ...£ 40

.. .. . Norton .............£ 15

The Madras System had a greater vogue in New Brunswick than in any other of the Provinces. In 1824 the schools under the Board numbered 39 and enrolled 4736 pupils. Eventually, however, the schools proved a failure, especially in rural communities, but they continued to exist in the larger centers until free schools robbed them of their pupils.

**Grammar Schools.** The first Grammar School to be opened in New Brunswick was at Fredericton in 1785. It was the outcome of a plan for an Academy originated by the Loyalists before they came to the Province. When the Province was divided for settlement, a large area was reserved near Fredericton for the school. In 1792 the Legislature gave the school a grant of £100 annually, which with the income from its lands, gave it an endowment of £200 a year. The founders of the institution looked forward to its incorporation as a Provincial College, and further notice will be taken of it under that head.

St. John was the largest settlement in the Province, and in 1805 it was provided with a Grammar School. The school had a Board of Directors, the President of which was, by law, the Rector of Trinity Church. The Board might admit eight free scholars. The Legislature gave the school a grant of £100 annually and the same sum for building purposes. The Board was accountable to the Legislature.

The same Act which established the Grammar School at St. John provided for two schools for each county, with the exception of St. John County, which was to have but one. These schools were to be held in each parish in a county in turn, until all the parishes had enjoyed them. The schools were under the direction and control of the Courts of General Sessions. A sum of £375 was appropriated for the support

4

of the masters, which gave each school £25. The Sessions appointed a Committee for each county to inspect the schools and report on them. They were to be inspected also by the clergyman or missionary residing in the parish where the school happened to be at the time. The schools taught English Language, Writing and Arithmetic. These were the first County Schools, and they were the forerunners of the County Grammar Schools.

After eleven years of the movable county schools, County Grammar Schools were established, somewhat after the pattern of the St. John Grammar School. Each of the Grammar Schools was given a Board of three or more Trustees, appointed by the Governor in Council. The Legislature gave a grant of £100 annually upon the assurance that the inhabitants of the county had provided a building and hired a master, and had raised £100 for the support of the school themselves. The studies prescribed were more advanced than those in the old county schools. They were; English Grammar, Latin, Greek, Orthography, Use of the Globes, Practical Mathematics, and other useful learning.

No radical changes were made in the arrangements for Grammar Schools for a long time. In 1829 it was made illegal for a clergyman in charge of a congregation to teach in a Grammar School. The grant continued to be £100, but it was found that the same sum required of the inhabitants was too much, and it was reduced to £50.

**The College of New Brunswick.** The Academy at Fredericton was incorporated as the College of New Brunswick by Provincial Charter in 1800. The President was in Holy Orders, and all the Professors had to be members of the Church of England, and the students had to subscribe to the Thirty-Nine Articles before taking their degrees.

In 1823 a petition was presented to the King asking that a Royal Charter be given the College. This was not granted until 1827. Under the new charter the name was changed to

5

King's College, and an endowment of £1000 was settled upon it from the Royal revenues on deposit in the Province. The Legislature gave a further endowment of £1100 annually. Although the name was new, the policies of the College remained the same. The members of the Board of Governors were all Anglicans, and the perpetual succession to the Presidency was vested in the Archdeacon of the Province. This insistence upon its control by the Church of England made the College very unpopular, although it was the only institution for higher learning in the Province.

During the period 1800—1846 the educational system of New Brunswick had made considerable progress. There were then elementary schools in most parishes, under the control of Parish Boards of Trustees. Provision had been made for the Trustees to report to the Courts of General Sessions, who compiled their reports from those of the Trustees and sent them to the Secretary of the Province, so,that the Legislature had a means of obtaining a limited amount of information about the schools. There was a Grammar School in each county, under a separate Board of Trustees, who were accountable only to the Legislature. Both kinds of schools received grants from the Provincial Treasury and depended upon subscription to augment this income.

While these developments were admirable, much was yet to be done. There was no central authority. The Court of General Sessions acted as a convenient agency for the collection of reports and the distribution of Parish School grants, but the Justices of the Peace were likely to be unsuited for educational supervision. The Trustees were appointed by the Sessions, as indeed all the parish officers were, so that other interests than those of education would be certain to govern their choice. The teachers were licensed "as by His Majesty's Royal Instructions is commanded," but they were untrained and inefficient. Finally, education was still a commodity to be paid for by those whose children received it, and for the poor, a charity.

**1847-1870.**
**Parish Schools.** The first Provincial Board of Education was authorized in 1847. The Board consisted of the Lieutenant Governor and the Executive Council. It had a Secretary but no Superintendent. The same Act which established the Board of Education empowered it to open a Training School for teachers with a Model School attached.

For the better licensing of teachers, three classes of licenses were made, and the Provincial grants paid according to the license held. The grants were: for a First Class License, £30; Second Class, £22; Third Class, £18. Before the grant would be paid to the teacher, the inhabitants had to subscribe and raise £10 for the support of the teacher, or provide board and lodging to this amount.

The Act of 1847 marked the establishment of a central authority. Henceforth the Parish Schools were governed not only by law, but by regulations of the Board, which could be made to suit changing conditions.

The First Training School was opened at Fredericton in 1847, and the following year another was started at St. John. Each school had a Board of Examiners attached to it, and upon the joint report of the Examiners and the Training School master the candidate's license depended. At first the term of training was six weeks, and later, twelve weeks.

Two inspectors were appointed by the Lieutenant Governor in Council. This was the beginning of official inspection in New Brunswick.

A further development in administration was made in 1852, when a Chief Superintendent of Parish Schools was appointed. At that time only one Training School was authorized, and it was at Fredericton. For the first time a distinction was made in the grants to male and female teachers, as follows:

| Males | First Class | £30 | Females | First Class | £20 |
|-------|-------------|-----|---------|-------------|-----|
| | Second Class | £20 | | Second Class | £18 |
| | Third Class | £18 | | Third Class | £14 |

These grants were in aid of the teacher. The upkeep of the school and any further salary paid the teacher were met by subscription. Districts and parishes were, however, permitted to assess themselves for the support of the schools, and to encourage this, 25% above the usual grant was offered to those communities adopting the assessment principle.

In 1858 new legislation was enacted for Parish Schools. Under it the Province was divided into four inspectoral districts. The Parish Trustees were then elected in each parish or town, where before they had been appointed. Each school district elected a School Committee of three persons. The Committees had very little authority. They could admit free scholars, reduce the fees to the poor, call meetings for the purpose of providing maps and other school equipment, and had control of any library belonging to the district.

The Legislative aid to teachers was slightly increased and the three classes of licenses continued. Among the duties laid upon the teacher was that of inculcating Christian principles in the minds of the pupils. The Board of Education could, by regulation, secure to all children the reading of the Bible in Parish Schools, and Roman Catholic children might read the Douay version without note or comment. These provisions were the foundation of a claim by the Roman Catholic that the Act of 1858 entitled them to teach their own religion in Parish Schools.

An interesting development in 1858 was the Superior School. In order to induce the people to improve their schools the Board of Education offered to pay an increased grant to one school in each parish if it merited a high rating. To be eligible the school had to have a competent teacher, for whose support the inhabitants had raised a sum of £50 or more. If then the inspector certified that the school was satisfactorily taught, the Provincial grant would equal the sum raised, up to £75.  In time the Superior School came to occupy a place between the Parish and the Grammar School.

**Grammar Schools**  In 1846 a special Committee of the Legislature consisting of Messrs. James Brown and John Gregory, and Dr. S. Z. Earle, reported on the condition of the Grammar Schools.  Their report stated that of the subjects prescribed to be taught, the number of pupils in each branch for the whole Province, with the exception of St. John and Northumberland Counties, was: Latin 20, Greek 3, Use of the Globes 2, Mathematics 7, English Gram nar 31.

There were, of course, pupils in the Grammar Schools studying other subjects than those mentioned, but these should have been in the Parish Schools.  It was so evident that the Grammar Schools were not serving the purpose for which they were intended that measures were immediately enacted to remedy the defects.

Under the new provisions the following subjects were prescribed: Orthography, Reading, Writing, Arithmetic, English Grammar, Geography, English Composition, Ancient and Modern History, Natural Philosophy, Natural History, the practical branches of Mathematics. Use of the Globes, Latin, Greek, and such other useful learning as was thought necessary.

Since some of the Grammar Schools had been taking children of elementary school age, a new provision made it necessary for them to have 15 pupils above the age of 10 years in daily attendance, and the teachers were required to keep a daily register.

The Trustees of the Grammar Schools had hitherto been required to report on the general state of the schools once a year.  They were now to inspect them every six months and to file a semi-annual report with the Provincial Secretary.

The grant to Grammar Schools was continued, and a penal clause added which made it possible for the Governor in Council to reduce the sum paid to any school if it appeared to be inefficiently conducted.

Nothing further was done for the Grammar Schools until they were brought under the control of the Board of Education in 1861, and they were then made subject to the inspection of the Superintendent.

**King's College.** King's College had not continued its operation long before complaints were made against its management and the exclusive character of its charter. The Governors of the institution resisted every effort of the Assembly to alter its charter, claiming it to be beyond their power. Finally, in 1854, a Commission was appointed by the Governor in Council to review the whole situation and to make recommendations. The members of the Commission were; the Hon. John H. Gray, the Hon John Simcoe Saunders, The Hon. James Brown, the Rev. Dr. Ryerson and Dr. J. W. Dawson. The report of the Commission was not implemented in its entirety. In 1859 the College was reorganized as the University of New Brunswick, and all religious barriers removed so that the institution became acceptable to all classes and denominations.

The period from 1847 to 1870 just reviewed was a period of reorganization. The formation of a central Board of Education and the appointment of a Superintendent were outstanding developments. Another feature of this period was the inauguration of training for teachers. An effort was made to arouse school districts by offering an increased grant to one school in each parish if it came up to certain requirements. The inspection was better than ever before. At first county inspectors were employed on part time, and later four inspectors for the whole Province gave all their attention to the Parish Schools.

The Grammar Schools were brought up to the level intended by law. They had become little better than Parish Schools. It was evident that the Trustees had performed their duties in a very perfunctory manner. The new arrangement provided a simple check on the character of the institutions. Eventually they came under the same regulations as the common schools.

The University of New Brunswick, after a long struggle, was finally put on a satisfactory basis. The governing authority was made non-denominational and the courses modernized, so that the prospects of its becoming a popular institution instead of an exclusive one, were bright, if late in achievement.

The period under review brought to a close the efforts to support schools by means of voluntary taxation. The Legislature at different times had endeavored to induce the people to tax themselves for school purposes, and it had offered premiums in the form of increased grants to those districts and parishes which would do it. In 1852, 25% additional grant was offered to any section adopting the assessment principle. In 1858, 10% was offered. In spite of these inducements not a single county, municipality or parish had supported its schools in this manner, and only here and there had a district done so.

**1871—1900** The outstanding event of 1871 was the passage of the Common Schools Act, which provided for free schools. Under the new Act, the support of elementary schools was derived from three sources; Provincial Aid to teachers; the County School Fund; District Assessment.

The parish as an administrative unit was abandoned and the school district adopted in its place. Each district elected three School Trustees at an annual School Meeting.

The teachers were classified according to the license held, as formerly. Inspection was continued, with fourteen inspectors.

Superior Schools were encouraged on the same plan as before.

A clause permitted the Trustees of a Grammar School to unite with the Trustees of a District School for the joint management of both, in which case both schools were to be free.

The last clause in the Act declared that all schools conducted under its provisions were to be non-sectarian.

A great deal of opposition to the whole Act arose because of its non-sectarian clause, and this opposition, as might have

11

been expected, came from the Roman Catholics. They argued that, since the Act of 1858 permitted instruction in Christian principles and allowed the Douay version of the Bible to be read by Roman Catholic children, this constituted a right to have denominational schools. As the Constitution of Canada secured to minorities any rights which they had enjoyed before Confederation, it was maintained that the Common Schools Act was unconstitutional because it deprived the Roman Catholics of the right to have denominational schools with government support. The matter was argued before the Supreme Court of New Brunswick, and before the Privy Council in England. In both cases the New Brunswick Act was upheld. In 1875, after the opposition had abated a little, a compromise was effected which made the Act more agreeable to the Roman Catholics. Under this arrangement the members of certain religious orders could qualify as teachers and the property owned by the Roman Catholic Church could be used by the Trustees for school purposes. All religious teaching was to be done outside of school hours.

**Common Schools** The old Parish Schools had never been graded, and one of the improvements in the Common Schools was evident in 1876, when there were 325 graded departments,being 25.5% of all the schools of the Province.

No uniform course of study had ever been pursued in the Parish Schools, and it was not until 1878 that one was prepared for the Common Schools. It came about in a curious way. The Act of 1871 provided that after five years from its inception, the Provincial Aid to teachers should be apportioned in part according to the class of license held, and in part according to the results of an examination conducted by an inspector. This scheme, called the Ranking System, was postponed until 1878. Before it could be enforced a uniform course of study for all the Common Schools was necessary, and it was first authorized in that year. The Ranking System came to an end in 1884.

There was no compulsory attendance law in New Brunswick until 1905. Earlier attempts to stimulate attendance relied upon prizes, which were bought by the Trustees out of school funds. The plan was not a marked success.

The progress of education in New Brunswick may be judged from the following:

| Year | Proportion of whole population in school. |
|------|-------------------------------------------|
| 1852 | 1 in 10.42 |
| 1862 | 1 in 8.92 |
| 1872 | 1 in 7.19 |
| 1882 | 1 in 6.09 |
| 1892 | 1 in 5.10 |
| 1902 | 1 in 5.75 |

**Superior Schools.** A Superior School in 1872 was one which had qualified itself by paying the teacher $200 or more and was then judged by an inspector to have been satisfactorily taught. When these conditions had been met, the Board of Education paid a grant equal to the sum raised for the teacher's salary, but not exceeding $300. There could be only one Superior School in any one parish. It soon appeared that this plan for the distribution of the Superior School Grant was a poor one, and a new basis was used in 1879. The grant was then made to depend upon the number of pupils annually certified by an inspector as having satisfactorily completed the work in Standard VIII of the Course of Study. The accommodations and equipment had to be up to the requirements of the Board. A lower Standard, VI, was required for the ungraded schools in rural districts. One-half the grant was paid to the teacher and one-half to the trustees.

In 1885 a new arrangement provided for one Superior School in each county for every 6000 inhabitants, but not more than one such school in any parish as a rule. The teacher received an annual grant of $250, provided the district paid him the same amount.

In 1887 a Course of Study was prepared for the Superior

and Grammar Schools. A Superior School in cities and incorporated towns, and towns having four graded departments, was required to give instruction in Standards IX and X, and if no higher Standard than X was taught, Standard VIII might be required, provided the average daily attendance was not more than 25. Should Standards IX, X, and XI be taught, no lower grade was included in the Superior School. In two- or three-department schools, the highest department was the Superior School.

Until 1895 the teachers of Superior Schools were required to hold a First Class License, and after that date the teacher had to hold a Superior School License as well.

In 1895 the number of Superior Schools was increased by the removal of the restriction which forbade the maintenance of more than one of these schools in a parish.

**Grammar Schools.** The Common Schools Act permitted the Grammar Schools to unite with the Common School in any district, and to be supported in the same manner. In 1884 the separate Grammar School Corporations were dissolved, and the property of the Grammar School was vested in the Board of Trustees for the district in which the school was situated. In 1885 the principal of a Grammar School received a grant of $350, and in 1897 this grant was paid to every Grammar School teacher, up to four in one school, provided that they were exclusively employed in teaching Grammar School grades. To be qualified for the grant, the teacher had to hold a Grammar School License·

In 1900 the Grammar Schools were graded, and had at least ten pupils above Grade VIII. Entrance to the High School grades was obtained by passing the High School Entrance Examinations. A Junior Leaving Examination was held for those desiring a certificate showing that they had completed Grade X. The University Matriculation Examination was on the work of Grades IX, X and XI. Entrance to the Normal School was gained by passing the Normal School Entrance Examination. All these examinations were set by a Provincial Board of Examiners under the control of the Board of Education.

The Board of Education was strengthened in 1871 by the addition of the President of the University of New Brunswick. In 1891 the Chief Superintendent was made, ex officio, the President of the University, and then the Chancellor of the University was made a member of the Board.

A number of educational institutions in operation in 1900, but not forming a part of the Provincial system of education remain to be mentioned. The largest of these were the Mount Allison institutions at Sackville, N. B. Mount Allison Academy was the oldest, having been founded in 1843. The Ladies' College dated back to 1854, and the University of Mount Allison to 1862.

The considerable Acadian population in New Brunswick had several institutions of their own, chief of which was the University of St. Joseph's College, at Memramcook, N. B. It was founded in 1864.

A number of private and denominational schools was flourishing in 1900. They were:

|  | Located at | Founded in |
| --- | --- | --- |
| St. Mary's Female Academy | Newcastle | 1864 |
| Congregation of Notre Dame | Caraquet | 1874 |
| St. Louis Convent School | St. Louis | 1874 |
| Academy of Our Lady of Snows | Campbellton | 1888 |
| Rothesay College for Boys | Rothesay | 1891 |
| Rothesay School for Girls | Rothesay | 1894 |

The Madras Schools had lost most of their pupils after 1872. In 1900 a part of their endowment was given to the Univeristy of New Brunswick and the rest to the Diocesan Synod of Fredericton for the support of schools under their control. In 1900 a few of the Madras Schools were still in operation.

An Institution for the Education of the Deaf and Dumb had been in operation since 1872. It was maintained by private subscriptions, a Provincial grant of $400 annually, a county grant of $60 per pupil, and by fees from parents.

There was no school for the blind in New Brunswick, but children from that Province were sent to the Nova Scotia School for the Blind at Halifax. Their expenses were borne at the rate per pupil of $75 from the Provincial Treasury, and $75 from the county sending the child.

The century of development which has been traced has had to deal almost entirely with elementary education. Although begun about the same time, the Grammar Schools underwent comparatively few changes. But for the Parish Schools the first attempts at support by taxation were made, and for them the Board of Education was evolved. The first Superintendent was also for Parish Schools. Finally, however, a system of education was evolved which included the Grammar Schools and was in close contact with the University, so that the year 1900 found New Brunswick with elementary schools in every district, which graded into the Superior and Grammar Schools, and these in turn fed the University.

---

Summary of the chief events in New Brunswick educational history.

1784    New Brunswick founded. Thomas Carleton the first Governor.
1800    The College of New Brunswick incorporated by Provincial Charter, at Fredericton.
1802    The first Legislative aid given to Parish Schools.
1805    The Grammar School at St. John founded.
1805    Two schools provided for each county, to be held in each parish in turn.
1816    County Grammar Schools established.
1816    First Act to permit Parish Schools to be supported by taxation. (This permission repealed in 1818).
1820    The Madras Board incorporated.
1827    A Royal Charter granted to the College of New Brunswick, and the name changed to King's College.
1829    The Legislature endowed King's College with £1100 annually.

1833 Trustees of Parish Schools made returns to the Sessions, and the latter to the Lieut. Governor.
The teachers made the first returns to the Clerks of the Peace.
1837 County Boards of Education established for the purpose of examining candidates for teacher's license.
1846 A Legislative Committee reported on the Grammar Schools.
1847 First Provincial Board of Education established.
First Training School for teachers, at Fredericton. (Another opened at St. John in 1848).
First inspectors appointed.
1852 Chief Superintendent of Parish Schools appointed. (Rev. James Porter).
1853 J. Marshall D'Avray appointed Chief Superintendent.
1854 A Commission appointed to investigate King's College.
1858 Henry Fisher appointed Chief Superintendent.
District School Committees provided.
Provision for one Superior School in each parish.
1859 King's College reorganized as the University of New Brunswick.
1860 John Bennet Ph. D.; Chief Superintendent.
1861 Grammar Schools brought under the control of the Board of Education, and the inspection of the Superintendent.
1871 Theodore H. Rand D.C.L., Chief Superintendent.
Free schools provided. The Act came into effect Jan. 1st, 1872.
1878 First Course of Study for Common Schools.
The Ranking System begun. Continued until 1884.
1883 William Crocket M.A., Chief Suprintendent.
1884 The separate Grammar School Corporations dissolved.
1887 A Course of Study for Superior and Grammar Schools provided.
1891 James R. Inch, M.A., LL. D., Chief Superintendent.
1891 The Chief Superintendent made ex officio President of the University.
1893 A joint Board of Examiners created.

# BIBLIOGRAPHY

Acts of the Assembly of New Brunswick respecting Education,
1802 to 1900.

Annual Reports of the Chief Superintendent of Education.
1853 to 1900.

Archives, Public, Ottawa

Carleton to Grenville, Aug. 20, 1790, Col. Cor. N. B.
vol. 2, p. 223.

Carleton to Dundas, June 2, 1792, Col. Cor. N. B.
vol. 2, p. 617.

Carleton to Grenville, March 9, 1793, Col. Cor. N. B.
vol. 3, p. 59.

Carleton to Portland, Aug. 4, 1800, Col. Cor. N. B.
vol. 8, p. 603.

Ward Chipman to Bathurst, May 15, 1823, Col. Cor. N.B.
vol. 27, p. 109.

Petition of Governor and Trustees of the College of New
Brunswick for a Royal Charter, 1823, Col. Cor. N. B.
vol. 27, p. 113,

Annual Report on the State of the Madras Schools in
New Brunswick for 1820 and 1822.


Allison, Leonard—Life of Dr. Oliver Arnold, and the Indian
College at Sussex. St. John. Sun Print Co. 1892.

Bowes, John A.—Historical Sketch of the St. John Grammar
School. St. John. Geo. W. Day. 1885.

Burtis, W. R. M.—New Brunswick as a Home for Emigrants.
St. John. Barnes and Co. 1860.

Chubb, Henry—Almanacks of New Brunswick 1812—1900·
St. John. Henry Chubb.

Educational Review, edited by G. U. Hay. 1892—1917, St.
John. Barnes and Co.

Educational Circular, nos. 2,3,5,6,7,10,11,13,14. Fredericton.
Printed for the Education Department by Barnes and Co.

Eaton, Arthur W.—The Church in Nova Scotia. New York.
Thomas Whittaker. 1892.

Fraser, The Hon. John J.,—Report of the Legislative Commission upon the Charges Relating to the Bathurst Schools, 1894.

Fisher, Peter—First History of New Brunswick. (Privately printed) 1825.

Gesner, Abraham—New Brunswick, with Notes for Emigrants. London. Simmons and Ward. 1847.

Hannay, James B.—History of New Brunswick. St. John. John A. Bowes, 1909.

Hannay, James B.—Life of Sir S. L. Tilley. St. John. (No printer given) 1897.

Hay, G. U.—Article in Canada and Its Provinces. vol. 14. Toronto. Glasgow, Brook and Co. 1914.

Inch, James R.—Article in Canada, an Encyclopaedia of the Country, vol. 3, edited by Castell Hopkins, Toronto. Linscott Publishing Co. 1898.

Journals of the Assembly of New Brunswick. 1846.

Kiernan, Bernard—Almanacks for New Brunswick, 1786-1823. St. John.

Lawrence, J. W.—Foot-Prints. St. John. J. and A. McMillan, 1883.

Maher vs. the Town Council of the Town of Portland, Argument before the Privy Council of Great Britain. 1874.

McFarlane, M. G.—Schools in Fredericton, an article in the Weekly Sun, Fredericton. 1893.

McLatchey, Josephine H.—A Legislative History of New Brunswick Education. vol. 29, no. 4, 1915 to vol. 30, no. 6, 1916 of the Educational Review.St.John. Barnes and Co.

Milner, W. C.—Our Lieutenant Governors. Pamphlet no. 160, N.B. Branch of Public Archives. St. John.N.B.

Munro, Alexander—New Brunswick, with a brief Outline of Nova Scotia and Prince Edward Island. Halifax. R. Nugent 1855.

New Brunswick Historical Society, Collections. vols. 1-12.

Newspapers,
> The newspapers mentioned below are in the New Brunswich Branch of the Public Archives of Canada, St. John, N. B.
> The St. John Gazette. 1791-1807, St. John.
> The Royal Gazette and New Brunswick Advertiser, 1786-1798; 1801-1826. St. John.
> The New Brunswick Courier. 1812-1827. St. John.

Pascoe, C. F.— Classified Digest of the Records of the Society for the Propagation of the Gospel in Foreign Parts. 1701-1892. London. Spottiswode and Co. 1893.

Perley, H. M.—A Handbook of Information for Emigrants to New Brunswick. London. Edward Stanford. 1857.

Raymond, W. O.—New Brunswick Schools of Olden Time. vol. 6, no. 7 to vol. 9 no. 7, Educational Review. St. John. Barnes and Co.

Raymond, W. O.—Winslow Papers, A. D. 1776—1826, St. John. The Sun Print Publishing Co. 1901.

Raymond, W. O.—The River St. John. St. John. John A. Bowes and Co. 1910.

Raymond, W. O.—Episodes in Local Church History. Published in the St.John Daily Telegraph at various times.1919

Regulations of the Board of Education, 1873.

Renaude and others, Judgment of the Supreme Court of New Brunswick upon the question of the constitutionality of the Common Schools Act, 1871. Hilary Term 1873.

Stewart, George, Jr.—The Story of the Great Fire in St. John N.B. Toronto. Belford Brothers. 1877.

Synoptic Report of the Proceedings of the Legislative Assembly of New Brunswick, 1852.

Watts, Samuel—Facts for the Information of Intending Emigrants about the Province of New Brunswick. St. John. The Carleton Sentinel. 1852.

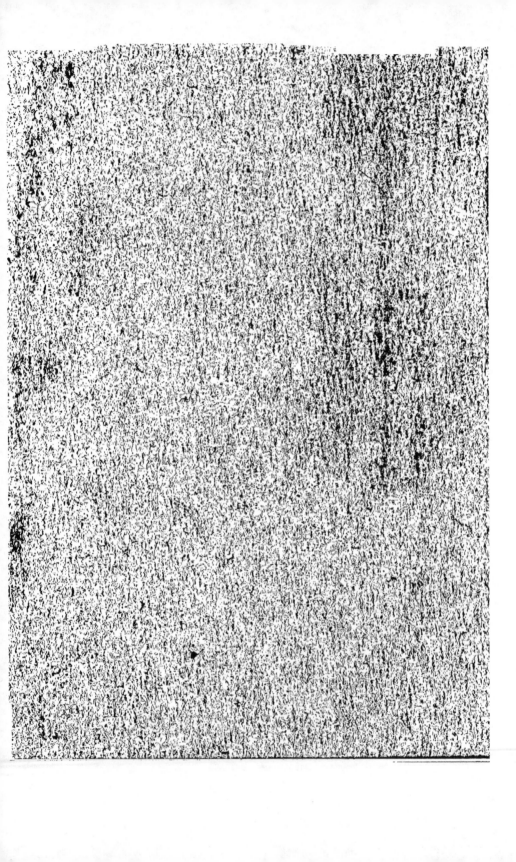

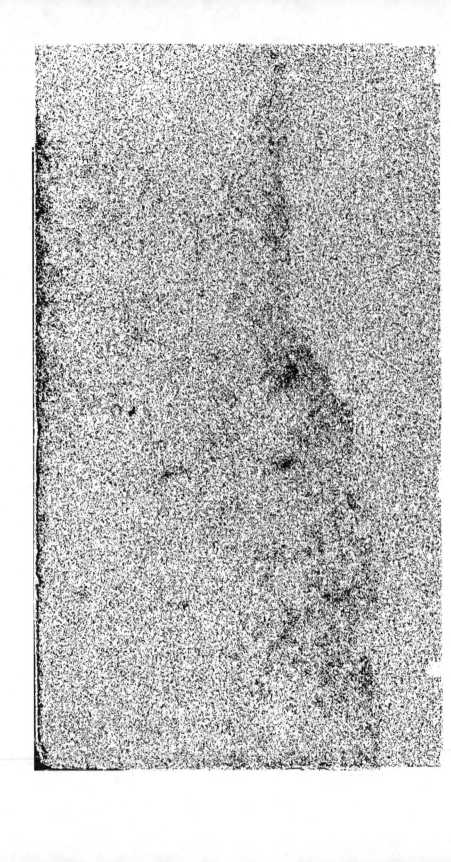

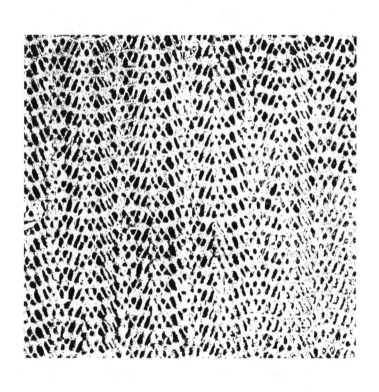

CPSIA information can be obtained
at www.ICGtesting.com
Printed in the USA
LVHW021248071118
596294LV00004B/702